D0996821

Aardman presents

Wensleydale
on road

Wallace
and Gromit's
Highway Code

First published 2003 by Boxtree
an imprint of Pan Macmillan Ltd
Pan Macmillan, 20 New Wharf Road, London N1 9RR
Basingstoke and Oxford
Associated companies throughout the world
www.panmacmillan.com

ISBN 0 7522 1571 X

Produced under license by Aardman Animations
© and ™ Aardman/Wallace and Gromit Ltd 2003

Text © Pan Macmillan Ltd 2003

9 8 7 6 5 4 3 2

A CIP catalogue record for this book is available from
the British Library.

Design by Dan Newman @ Perfect Bound Ltd
Text by Annie Schafheitle and Natalie Jerome

Printed by Proost, Belgium

Aardman presents

Wallace and Gromit's Highway Code

B◯XTREE

Wensleydale on road

You can have 15 minor faults before you fail your driving test. Luckily, thinking your instructor smells of cheese isn't one of them.

Try your brakes

Always ensure you have enough tread on your slippers to grip the brake pedal. Don't trust others to do this for you.

When driving in the country, watch out for sheep crossing. Shaun wondered if he should have worn the fluorescent vest for added visibility.

Show respect to truckers.
If it weren't for them,
petrol stations wouldn't
stock chicken and
ham slices.

**Gromit is starting to
think he should have
taken the bus.**

Diplomacy on the roads is very important. This is not the way to query a parking ticket.

**REDUCE
SPEED
NOW**

Be considerate at all
times. If you can see the
driver in front of you
clearly, you're too close.

Practice makes perfect, so Gromit takes a dry run before heading out on Wallace's scooter.

**Stay alert!
Stuck in the middle
of the road, Shaun
regretted not using
the zebra crossing...**

Don't be put off if your driving instructor is a little frosty.

On long-distance journeys, make sure you take regular breaks, or you may find yourself with spots (or sheep) before your eyes...

Take pride in your vehicle. Wallace prepares to wax on, wax off.

Try your brains

Be careful when practising for your driving test at home. Wallace often mistakes Feathers for a gearstick.

Shaun was starting to feel dizzy after taking the roundabout sign too literally.

Plan for emergencies. The ladder always came in handy as a make-shift bridge.

Watch out for aircraft. Gromit was ready for a showdown before realising penguins can't fly.

Preston's collar was restricting his ability to look both ways.

Try to remain calm at traffic lights. Shaun's chewing always becomes more vigorous when the lights turn green.

Fog

Take extra care driving in difficult weather. Gromit watches out for penguins in the mist.

School

To be a good driver you need to know your highway code thoroughly.

Keep your eyes on
the road. Feathers
hopes there are no
leaves on the line.

Remember to read the REAL Highway Code before your driving test.

Wensleydale
on road